# The Social Skills Picture Book
## for High School and Beyond

By Jed Baker, Ph.D.

Future Horizons, Inc.

# The Social Skills Picture Book
for High School and Beyond

All marketing and publishing rights guaranteed to and reserved by:

**FUTURE HORIZONS** INC.

721 W. Abram Street
Arlington, TX 76013

800-489-0727

817-277-0727

817-277-2270 Fax

Website: www.FHautism.com
E-mail: info@FHautism.com

ISBN 10: 1-932565-35-3

ISBN 13: 978-1-932565-35-5

# Acknowledgements

I wish to thank all the dedicated students and their families who participated in the creation of the pictures for this book. I would also like to acknowledge Millburn School District in New Jersey for allowing me to take pictures in the school setting and for having the foresight to hire a social skills consultant to create school-based social skills training programs for their district.

Kelly Gilpin, my editor, must also be mentioned, as she made sure the pictures actually came together to form a book.

Finally, my family deserves praise for their patience as I sat at the computer at times when they wanted to talk and play. They also agreed to pose for some of the pictures and did not even request a modeling fee.

# Contents

# Foreword

After the publication of the *Social Skills Picture Book* (Baker, 2001), I received many calls and emails from families and teachers telling me that their students seemed highly motivated and interested in learning from the pictures. This feedback was certainly what I had hoped for, as it had been my experience with the students with whom I had worked. Then I began to receive more and more calls and emails asking if I could put together a similar picture book for older students.

Although many teens liked looking at the pictures in the previous publication (which depicts mostly elementary-aged children), the teens could not easily relate to those younger students. Thus I began to make picture books for older, high school students, using the more sophisticated situations that these students often face, including peer conflicts, dating, employment, and classroom situations.

I sincerely wish for you and your teens to have fun using these picture books and making your own. To build the desire to socialize, lessons must be enjoyable. For more information on skill lessons for high school students and ideas to make lessons fun, the interested reader might also want to read *Preparing for Life: The Complete Guide to Transitioning to Adulthood for those with Autism and Asperger's Syndrome* (Baker, 2005). That book contains over seventy written skill lessons. A subset of those skills has been depicted here in picture form to create the *Social Skills Picture Book for High School and Beyond*.

# PART ONE ■

# The Autism Spectrum and the Importance of Visual Aids

## Asperger's Syndrome and Autism Spectrum Disorders

*Autism Spectrum Disorders* (also known as Pervasive Developmental Disorders) constitute a wide range of symptoms that affect an individual's sensory, cognitive, motor, language, and social-emotional development. Asperger's Syndrome, autism, and Pervasive Developmental Disorder–Not Otherwise Specified (PDD-NOS) are some of the most common Autism Spectrum Disorders.

The autism spectrum is considered a "spectrum" because the individuals who comprise it vary greatly from each other. Intellectually, some fall in the mentally retarded range while others clearly fall in the superior intellectual range. Asperger's Syndrome and High-Functioning Autism involve, by definition, individuals with average to above average intellectual ability and better communication skills than those with more "classic" autism who tend to have lower intellectual functioning and more communication difficulties. Those who have symptoms of an Autism Spectrum Disorder but do not meet the full criteria for a specific diagnosis like autism or Asperger's Syndrome are typically given the diagnosis PDD-NOS. This actually represents the largest category of individuals on the spectrum, which means that although we can identify individuals on the spectrum, the diagnostic process is not yet good at making specific differential diagnoses among Autism Spectrum Disorders.

Current diagnostic criteria describe Autism Spectrum Disorders as involving difficulties in three general areas: (a) qualitative impairment in social interactions (e.g., impairment in responding to or initiating interactions with others, or failure to form peer relationships), (b) qualitative impairment in verbal and nonverbal communication (e.g., no mode of communication, or impairment in the ability to initiate or sustain conversations), and (c) restricted, repetitive, and stereotyped patterns of behavior, interests or activities (e.g., preoccupation with restricted patterns of interest, or inflexible adherence to nonfunctional routines or rituals) (American Psychiatric Association, 1994).

Problems with social interaction can include difficulties initiating or responding to conversation, difficulties using or responding to nonverbal gestures (e.g., pointing out objects), lack of or inconsistent eye contact, impairment in responding to others' feelings, difficulties working cooperatively with peers, and subsequent failure to develop peer relationships. Understanding what to do or say in social situations is a core concern for autistic individuals.

Communication problems range from no ability to communicate and use language to more subtle difficulties with the flow of conversation and social communication (pragmatic language). Some classically autistic individuals may have difficulties understanding the meanings of most words and may show little spontaneous language communication. In contrast, those with High-Functioning Autism and Asperger's may appear to have excellent command of language in terms of their ability to express themselves and understand others, yet they may have great trouble with the flow of social conversation, talking *at* people instead of *with* people, relaying factual information or phrases memorized from TV shows without responding to what their listener is saying or doing. Thus individuals with Asperger's may have extensive vocabularies, but difficulty using it in a fluid way to make conversation in social situations. High-functioning individuals, like those with more language difficulties, may also have trouble with abstract language and tend to interpret things literally. For example, if a teacher said, "Don't let the cat out of the bag," a literal interpretation would have a student looking for a cat and a bag. In addition, many students with autism may have trouble processing language when there are competing sights and sounds. Thus using language alone to explain complicated material may sometimes be less effective than supplementing the explanation with concrete visual information that supports the verbal explanation (Quill, 1995).

Repetitive and ritualistic behaviors reflect a preference for sameness and repetition with regards to interests, daily routine, and body movements. Many youngsters with autism develop a fascination with a particular area of interest and elaborate on that interest to the exclusion of learning about new things. For example, I knew a youngster who became obsessed with vacuum cleaners and was reluctant to attend to or talk about anything else. Many individuals with autism also exhibit nonfunctional routines that appear superstitious in nature. One individual I worked with had to hang every picture in the house at a crooked angle before he could use the toilet. Other students may not have nonfunctional routines, but prefer that their daily routines occur the same way all the time and may become very anxious or upset when changes or transitions are introduced. Youngsters may also demonstrate repetition in their use of language (repeating the same phrase over and over) or in their physical movements (e.g., repetitive hand flapping, body rocking, or twirling around).

Because of the difficulties individuals with Autism Spectrum Disorders have in negotiating social situations and handling changes in their environment, many students experience stress, frustration and anxiety on an almost constant basis (Kim, Szatmari, Bryson, Streiner, & Wilson, 2000; Myles & Southwick, 1999). Wanting to interact with another student but not knowing how, not understanding the change in teacher directions for a new challenging task, hearing other students laugh around them, and not knowing whether they are the target of the joke—these are all stressful situations that youths with Autism Spectrum Disorders experience daily.

Despite this level of stress, it is important to point out the emotional variability among students with Autism Spectrum Disorders. Some students rarely seem to get upset, as they may handle their stress by withdrawal and go virtually unnoticed. Others present with additional anxiety disorders (e.g., Obsessive-Compulsive Disorder, Social Phobia, or Panic Disorder). Some students seem to be constantly frustrated, impulsive, and have frequent tantrums. Many of these individuals may also be diagnosed with Attention Deficit Disorder or a Mood Disorder (e.g., Bipolar Disorder). Although students may react and cope with the stresses in their lives quite differently, they may share a similar reason for experiencing high levels of stress, as described below.

Given the variety of symptoms and levels of intellectual functioning among individuals with Autism Spectrum Disorders, a number of researchers have theorized about the core underlying problem within the disorders. Three, perhaps related, theories have received the most attention:

1. Frith (1989) suggests that autistic individuals lack the ability to simultaneously integrate the multiple language, social and emotional messages typically present in social situations. Something about their neurological functioning makes it difficult to assimilate and organize all the pertinent information. Since most social situations have multiple levels of sensory input, autistic individuals do not always fully grasp what is happening or how to respond. Instead, they may attend to and process only a fragment of the social experience, resulting in repetitive and atypical social behavior.

2. Baron-Cohen (1995) suggests that the core problem is the inability to understand the thoughts and feelings of others, a process termed "theory of mind." Thus, autistic individuals have difficulty taking other people's perspectives.

3. Hobson (1996) suggests that autism involves the inability to perceive and understand emotional expressions. This would then lead to difficulties in perspective taking and subsequent problems in social interaction.

These three theories can be considered complementary. Both Baron-Cohen and Hobson's theories suggest that autistic individuals cannot easily empathize with or understand another person's view of the world. Frith's theory helps explain why. The inability to simultaneously integrate information about what is happening in a social situation makes it difficult to imagine what others might be thinking and feeling. To take another's perspective, one has to synthesize information about the other person (e.g., the person's recent past experiences and preferences), along with what is happening to the person.

Most social skills rely on the ability to mentally adopt another person's perspective. For example, knowing why to say hello when you greet someone is based on understanding how others might think or feel if you ignore them rather than greet them. Knowing when to stop talking, take turns, respond to others' initiations, compromise, help others, or share, all come naturally when a person can easily take another's perspective. However, these social skills do not come naturally to autistic individuals, and must be taught explicitly if they are going to be mastered. The Social Skills Pictures that follow attempt to do just that—break down social skills into their components and make explicit what to do and say in social situations, and why.

## The Importance of Visual Aids in Teaching Those with Autism Spectrum Disorders

As described earlier, autistic individuals often have language processing difficulties including: (a) for classically autistic individuals, difficulties comprehending language, (b) for high-functioning individuals, difficulties with abstract language, and (c) for many autistic individuals, difficulty attending to verbal explanations when there is competing visual and auditory information. Visual aids can often facilitate both attention and language comprehension.

The benefits of visual aids to facilitate greater understanding and comprehension among autistic students have been well documented (e.g., Quill, 1995). Even most students without disabilities benefit from visual aids that back up a verbal explanation. This is because visual pictures can (a) make abstract verbal concepts more concrete, (b) remain stable over time whereas auditory information can be missed as students' attention fluctuates, and (c) provide a more powerful means to engage attention.

The Social Skills Picture Books use a primarily visual strategy to teach social skills. Although the picture books may benefit "typical" students, they will be particularly helpful for those with auditory/language processing difficulties, difficulties in abstract thinking, and for those with difficulties sustaining attention. This includes individuals on the autistic spectrum, those with Attention Deficit/Hyperactivity Disorders, and individuals with learning disabilities.

When it comes to teaching social skills, pictures present another advantage over traditional verbal explanations. Pictures allow one to depict and highlight the nonverbal social cues that many individuals on the spectrum may not intuitively understand. For example, facial expressions, gestures, eye-contact, and body posture that correspond to different feelings and attitudes can be presented visually in a way that verbal explanation cannot convey. As the saying goes, "a picture is worth a thousand words."

# About Social Skills Picture Books

## What Are Social Skills Picture Books?

The Social Skills Picture Books depict, step by step, teens demonstrating various social skills. The books are like cartoon strips, yet they are composed of digital pictures of actual students combined with text and cartoon bubbles to denote what the students are saying as they engage in the skills. The pictures show, for each step of a skill, the right way (and sometimes the wrong way) to act, along with accompanying text that explains what to do.

As described earlier, the picture books attempt to compensate for the inherent difficulties many autistic individuals share. The picture books make explicit what to do and say in social situations. In addition, by utilizing a picture format, they compensate for language processing difficulties and distractibility, making abstract concepts more concrete and stable.

Reading the picture books is not a substitute for actually practicing the skills. The picture books are tools to use in the initial acquisition of skills and should be followed with actual practice of the skills in the situations in which they are needed. If the goal is for a student to demonstrate a skill in a particular situation, then ultimately the student will need to repeatedly practice that skill in that situation. However, before students can physically practice a skill, they need some understanding of what to do. The picture books can facilitate that initial understanding.

The reason one performs a skill is often because it achieves a desired outcome. The picture books help individuals visualize (a) the positive outcomes of performing a skill and (b) how people think and feel in response to their behaviors.

## Who Should Use Picture Books?

The picture books will benefit most "typical" students by engaging attention and breaking down abstract skills into more concrete steps. It will be particularly helpful for those who have difficulties with auditory/language processing, abstract thinking, and sustaining attention. This includes individuals on the autistic spectrum as well as those with Attention Deficit/Hyperactivity Disorders and/or multiple learning disabilities.

## How to Use the Picture Books

Using the picture books involves the four stages described below: (1) initial instruction, (2) role-playing the skill, (3) reviewing the skill steps with corrective feedback, and (4) generalization. The first three stages can be repeated many times, such that one could go back to stage 1 after stage 3. These stages are quite similar to the stages of "structured learning," described by Goldstein and colleagues in their "skills streaming" series (McGinnis & Goldstein, 1997). Structured learning contains four components: didactic instruction (explanation of the skill steps), modeling, role-playing with feedback, and practice for generalization. The difference is that didactic instruction and modeling stages are replaced by using the picture books. Thus there is less reliance on verbal instruction and instructor modeling.

## Initial Instruction

The initial instruction involves an instructor or the students themselves reading and reviewing the skill steps page by page. An instructor can show each picture and read each skill step in order, describing what the individuals are doing, thinking and feeling. The instructor can go through each page of a particular skill numerous times and then ask the student to tell what is happening in each picture. The instructor would ask questions such as, "What is happening here? What is the first step? How is he feeling? What is he saying? What happens next?" For students who cannot describe what is happening, they can be asked to show each step (e.g., "Show me 'step one' where they make eye-contact. Now show me where they wait for a pause. Is this the right way or wrong way to say excuse me?")

## Should You Teach the "Wrong Way" to Enact a Skill?

The instructor may choose not to explain or show the wrong way to enact a skill step and instead just focus on the right way to engage in the skill. The instructor may cover up the picture of the wrong way when going through the picture books. The potential disadvantage of reviewing the wrong way is that some students are so entertained by the inappropriate behavior that they may continually perform it the wrong way for their own or others' amusement. On the other hand, the advantage of demonstrating the wrong way is two-fold: (a) certain skills will be much better understood when both the right and wrong way are shown, and (b) students who are reluctant to role-play may be more likely to try if they can role-play the wrong way first because then they do not have to fear making a mistake.

The bottom line is that instructors must know their students. Those youngsters who show a lot of "silly" attention-seeking behaviors are not among those who should be given the opportunity to role-play a skill the wrong way.

## Role-playing the Skill

During the practice stage, the student is asked to act out the skill steps in the right order. Here the instructor role-plays the skill as shown in the book, prompting the student through each skill step. This might be best to do with two instructors or one instructor and two students. This way, the instructor can avoid participating in the role-play directly and act as a coach to help the students through the skill steps as they are acted out with the other role-play participant.

Role-play situations can begin with the exact situations that are depicted in the picture books, and then can be varied to address the situations most relevant to the students in their daily lives.

## Reviewing the Skill/Corrective Feedback

After each role-play, the instructor provides feedback about whether each step was followed correctly. Feedback should always begin with what was performed correctly along with ample praise. When a step was conducted incorrectly, the instructor should avoid telling the student directly that they performed it incorrectly. Instead, the instructor should give the corrective feedback by saying something like, "In this step, here is what I want you to do to perform the step even better." As the feedback is given, the appropriate page and skill step of the picture book can be shown and modeled to demonstrate the correct way to perform the skill. The corrective feedback should be given until the student is able to demonstrate the skill step correctly.

The process of explaining the picture book, role-playing the skill, and providing corrective feedback can be repeated over and over until the student is able to demonstrate the skill steps without prompting through each step. At this point, efforts should be made to promote generalization of the skill (see Chapter 3).

## Making Your Own Picture Books

The books have two important uses and functions. First, as described earlier, students can learn the steps of the skills before they role-play or enact skills. They serve as excellent tools for acquisition and rehearsal of skills at home or in school. Secondly, students can actively participate in the creation of these books by posing for pictures and by assembling the books on paper or a computer. The benefits are doubled for students who create their own books. They have the opportunity to role-play the skills during the picture taking, then have their attention drawn to a permanent, highly appealing record of themselves engaged in the skill.

For those teens who are resistant to learning skills, participation in making picture books presumably to "help others" can increase their motivation. So for students who say, "I don't need to learn any skills," one can ask, "Will you help me make picture books to teach others?" Then they may learn the skills they need without the "stigma" of receiving help for themselves.

In making your own social skills picture book, you need to consider (a) the target skill, (b) how to task analyze the skill, (c) what perceptions, thoughts, or feelings you want to highlight for the student, and (d) how to put the book together.

Parents, teachers, or students can **identify target skills**. Individualized skills can be patterned after one of the 28 skills depicted in this book. On the other hand, one may develop a new skill that is based on a student's particular problematic behavior in a specific situation. Any time a student misbehaves, one can ask why or what was the student trying to achieve? Trying to answer the "why" questions, to determine the function of a behavior, is called a functional assessment (see Durand, 1990). Often the function of a problem behavior is to escape some task, get attention, provide self-stimulation, demand a tangible reward, displace anger from a previous situation, or seek retaliation. Whatever the function of the misbehavior, a crucial strategy to remedy the problem is to teach the student a more appropriate way to get what he or she wants (a replacement skill). The replacement skill is what we may want to target for a picture book. Some ideas for replacement skills to teach for each proposed function of behavior is shown below:

| FUNCTION | INAPPROPRIATE BEHAVIOR | REPLACEMENT SKILLS |
|---|---|---|
| Escape | Tantrums, physical or verbal aggression, refusals | Trying when it's hard, asking for a break, negotiating more time, asking for help, dealing with fear of trying something new, dealing with mistakes |
| Attention | Teasing, disruptive noises, inappropriate jokes or comments, complaints of being hurt | Initiating conversation, joining a conversation, asking for help, knowing when to stop being funny |
| Self-Stimulation | Rocking, hand flapping, twirling | Performing the self-stimulatory behavior in a less disruptive way, alternative ways to relax or self-soothe |
| Tangible reward | Tantrums for a privilege, refusing to cooperate with anything until reward is given | Accepting no for an answer or learning to wait for what you want, negotiating skills |
| Displaced anger | Verbal or physical aggression directed at the wrong person, refusal to cooperate with any instructions | Identifying common sources of anger (e.g., someone yelled at or reprimanded you), asserting yourself with others rather than acting it out, conflict resolution |
| Retaliation | Teasing back, hitting back, stealing from someone who upset you | Dealing with teasing, conflict resolution, asserting yourself |

**Task analyzing** the skill you have chosen to target means breaking down that skill into simpler component steps. How much to break down a skill depends on the student. If you break down a skill too far it will be cumbersome to learn. Likewise, failure to break it down enough will lead to the student having difficulty learning the skill. As an example, imagine you were teaching "complimenting" as a skill and one of the steps was, "Say nice things about how the person looks." Some students would know what "nice things" are, but other students would need that broken down further. For example, we might show that nice things use words

"I like _____" and "You are really good at _____." Then we could ask the student to say nice things. How far to break things down depends on the response of the student. If he or she is not learning or understanding the steps, then the skill needs to be broken down into smaller, more concrete steps.

**Highlighting perceptions** needs to be a part of the picture books. The better the student understands what people are thinking and feeling, the more likely he or she is to understand why to enact the skill. We want to demonstrate for the student what is "in it for him or her" to engage in the skill. Is it because it makes the other person happy and then the other person will give you something you want, or work with you again? For example, "accepting no" shows that others feel good when you accept no and then may give you what you want later.

In **putting the books together**, there are several choices. First one should map out the skill steps and what pictures you will need. Then you can pose students for the pictures while going through each skill step. You can first model what to do in the picture, then ask the student to do it. Do not worry if the student does not understand the skill fully as the learning of the skill will be reinforced after the picture books are created. You may be able to create these picture books with a variety of suitable photograph software programs. Alternatively, pictures can be taken with a non-digital camera and pasted to paper. Bubbles and text can then be hand written or typed onto colored paper and pasted onto the pictures. Students can not only pose for the pictures, but can also participate in the cutting, pasting and assembling of the picture book skills. In fact, the exercise of sequencing the skill in the right order can be made into a game to further enhance the understanding of the skill steps.

Most importantly, the assembling of picture books with or without the student should be fun. If you are enjoying yourself, you are less likely to feel burnt out by challenging behaviors and your positive attitude will be translated into better training with the students. So have fun and be creative.

# Generalization of Skills

Generalization refers to the ability to perform a skill in situations beyond the training session and to maintain the skill over time. Gresham et al. (2001) describe three aspects of skill deficits that are related to generalization problems: skill acquisition, performance levels, and fluidity. Acquisition refers to knowledge of skill steps. Students need to know the steps to later demonstrate them when needed. Performance refers to whether the student actually demonstrates the skill steps at acceptable levels of frequency in the situations in which the skills are needed. Fluidity refers to the ability to perform the skill steps accurately and without awkwardness. Fluidity often means that the individual no longer has to "consciously think through the steps" but can actually perform the skill "automatically" without much effort.

Knowing whether a skill deficit is an acquisition, performance or fluidity problem determines what strategies to use to remedy the deficit. Acquisition problems require more skill lesson instruction. Performance deficits require better use of antecedent control (cuing and prompting of skills) and reinforcement (praising and rewarding skill use, including contrived rewards or natural rewards). Fluidity problems require high levels of practice and repetition with corrective feedback (Gresham et al., 2001).

To realistically practice and repeat skill steps enough to achieve adequate levels of performance and fluidity, it is unlikely that one can generalize many new skills at once. In my experience, generalization occurs when individuals are reminded about or rehearse no more than one to three new skills every day for several months. Although individuals can learn the concept of many more skills during skill lessons, they may only be able to generalize one to three new skills at a given time. As Gresham et al. (2001) recommend, skills training has to be more intense and frequent than what has been typical in the literature. One 8-12 week course will not do. Focusing on one to three skills, practicing them daily in natural situations for several months at a time is likely to yield much better generalization results.

After students have acquired knowledge of skills, there are three strategies to help achieve adequate performance and fluidity of the skills: **priming** before the situation in which the skills are needed, frequent **facilitated opportunities to practice** the skills in natural situations (facilitated means someone can coach the student by prompting learning opportunities), and **review** of how skills were used after the situation in which they were needed. Practice in the natural situation is key to being able to later demonstrate those skills in same or similar situations.

## Priming

Priming involves some reminder to the individual of what the skill steps are "just prior" to needing the skill. For example, just before going on a job interview, an individual might go over how to answer anticipated questions. Or just prior to starting a frustrating task at school or at work, the individual might review options for trying when it's hard. Priming can be verbal or supplemented by a visual aid like the picture book. Verbal priming involves someone verbally explaining the skill steps prior to the situation in which they will be needed. Cue cards, behavior charts, or copies of the picture books can serve as visual aids that depict the skill steps.

**Cue cards**. If students want to change their behavior but can't remember the skill steps, then cue cards or copies of the picture books may be ideal. We might write one to three skills on an index card and laminate it. Then we might ask a parent, teacher, job coach, or the student him- or herself to review the skill steps prior to the situation in which it will be needed. Although it would be ideal for the student to see the skill steps immediately prior to the situation, this may not always be practical. Instead the parent, teacher, job coach, or student might review the skill once in the morning prior to school or work, once at lunch and then again at the end of the day, so that the student has to at least think about the skill three times per day. This kind of sustained awareness of the targeted skills on a daily basis over the course of several months often allows students to remember the skill without reminders from others.

**Behavior charts**. Behavior charts can be used just like cue cards. No rewards are given; rather, the chart itself simply serves as a reminder to use the skill. The student may rate him- or herself, or a teacher, parent, or job coach can rate the student after a specified period of time (serving as a reminder for the next period of time). If a student has not fully agreed to try a new skill and thus is lacking in "intrinsic" motivation to perform the skill, then the behavior chart can be used as a *reward* chart by making external rewards contingent on demonstrating certain targeted skills. In this case, self-monitoring may not work and teachers, parents, or employers may need to do the monitoring.

## Facilitated Opportunities

In order to practice the new skills, students need opportunities. Sometimes those opportunities are naturally built into the day. For example, a student learning to deal with frustrating work may always have his or her share of challenging work to do during the day. Other times, the practice opportunities need to be carefully planned or created. For example, a student who never initiates conversation with anyone may be asked to call someone on the phone once per day or join others for lunch and initiate conversation once during lunch period. School staff may need to create a lunch bunch group in which an adult staff member facilitates conversation among a small group of students at lunch. Without such efforts by adults, some students would not engage in conversation in the larger lunch room.

For students who have difficulty working cooperatively in groups, scheduling group projects in one or more of their classes each semester will serve as a natural opportunity to practice "working cooperatively in groups." The only difference from a typical group project is that these students might be primed ahead of time as to how to work together in groups.

Those working on job skills should have real opportunities to get a job, try to maintain it, and, if necessary, exit the job appropriately. There is no substitute for on-the-job training. Skill deficits can then be categorized as problems with skill acquisition, performance levels, or fluidity and then remedied through more instruction, better cueing and use of incentives, or more repetition to develop fluidity.

## Review After Skill Use

After situations have occurred in which skills were needed, the student's performance can be reviewed to increase awareness of the skill. If a student is on a reward chart, the reason why the student received the reward (or not) should be reviewed with him or her to enhance learning. For students not on reward charts, the situation can be reviewed verbally or with the help of the cue card of skills described earlier.

In reviewing past situations, care should be taken not to "shame" a student with examples of what they did incorrectly. The following steps can be taken to keep the review constructive and avoid negative judgments:

1. Ask the student what happened in the situation and how he or she dealt with the situation. Avoid judgments about any incorrect ways to handle the situation.

2. Explore how people felt and thought in the situation and discuss what happened as a result of the way the student dealt with the situation.

3. Explore what else he or she could have done in the situation.

4. Finally the student should be asked what he or she might do in the future to "handle the situation even better." Note the positive phrasing here. The adult can add some ideas "to make the future situations even more successful."

Some students may not be able to tolerate any discussion about a past situation as it may make them ashamed. In these instances, it is best not to mention what did happen, but rather what to do if a similar situation comes up again. Wait until sometime after the event when the student is calm and then say, "I wanted to talk to you about something that may happen in the future" (with no mention of the negative event that recently occurred). "Sometime you may _____," and the adult can continue to describe a situation that may occur and how the student might want to handle it. Using this method, the student still benefits from a review of a past event, although only the adult helping the student has done the review. From the student's point of view, this is just information to be used for the future.

# References

Baker, J. E. (2001). *Social Skill Picture Book*. Arlington, TX: Future Horizons, Inc.

Baker, J. E. (2005). *Preparing for Life: The complete guide to transitioning to adulthood for those with Autism and Asperger's Syndrome*. Arlington, TX: Future Horizons, Inc.

Baron-Cohen, S. (1995). Mindblindness. Cambridge, MA: The MIT Press.

Durand, V.M. (1990). *Severe Behavior Problems: A functional communication training approach*. New York: Guilford Press.

Frith, U. (1989). *Autism: Explaining the enigma*. Oxford, England: Blackwell.

Gresham, F.M., Sugai, G., & Horner, R. H. (2001). "Interpreting outcomes of social skills training for students with high-incidence disabilities." *Exceptional Children, 67*, 331-344.

Hobson, R.P. (1996). *Autism and the Development of the Mind*. Mahwah, NJ: Lawrence Erlbaum Associates.

Kim, J. A., Szatmari, P., Bryson, S. E., Streiner, D. L., & Wilson, F. J. (2000). "The prevalence of anxiety and mood problems among children with autism and Asperger Syndrome." *Autism, 4,* 117-132.

Myles, B. S., & Southwick, J. (1999). *Asperger Syndrome and Difficult Moments: Practical solutions for tantrums, rage, and meltdowns*. Shawnee Mission, KS: Autism Asperger Publishing Company.

Quill, K. A. (Ed.) (1995), *Teaching Children with Autism*. Albany, NY: Delmar Publishing.

McGinnis, E. & Goldstein, A. (1997). *Skillstreaming the Elementary School Child: New strategies and perspectives for teaching prosocial skills*. Champaign, IL: Research Press.

# PART TWO

# NONVERBAL CUES/ BODY LANGUAGE

## RELATED SKILLS

# Welcome Versus Unwelcome

- Try to show a welcoming look when friends come near.

- When others show a welcoming look, approach them.

- When others show an unwelcoming look, you may want to go elsewhere.

# Try to show a welcoming look when friends come near.

**Right Way**

They all welcome her by turning towards her and waving.

**Wrong Way**

They all look away and pretend they do not see her. That makes her feel bad and not want to be with them.

# When others show a welcoming look, approach them.

They ask him to join them.

So he does.

When others show an unwelcoming look,
you may want to go elsewhere.

The girl is not comfortable with the
boy being right next to her.

So he moves farther away.

# Knowing When to Stop Talking

■ Look for signs of interest in others as you speak.

■ If someone looks bored, ask if they want to hear more.

■ If they do not want to hear more:

— Stop talking or

— Ask about them.

# Look for signs of interest in others as you speak.

The young man is speaking and the young woman seems interested.

# If someone looks bored, ask if they want to hear more.

**Right Way**

The young man sees that she looks bored, so he asks her if she wants to hear more.

**Wrong Way**

The young man does not see that she looks bored, so he continues to talk.

■ If they do not want to hear more, then stop talking or ask what they want to talk about.

**Right Way**

The young man stops talking and asks about her.

**Wrong Way**

The young man does not realize she is bored and continues to talk. Now she wants to leave.

# Listening Position

■ Face the person and look towards their eyes.

■ Quiet Hands and Feet. Stay still.

■ Quiet Mouth. Don't talk while others are talking.

# ■ Show a listening position when talking with friends.

**Right Way**

They are facing him, looking towards his eyes, with quiet hands and feet, and not interrupting.

**Wrong Way**

She is looking away from him.

# Show a listening position in class.

**Right Way**

They are facing the teacher, staying still, and not interrupting.

**Wrong Way**

They are not facing the teacher, and are moving around and talking during class.

## Show a listening position during a job interview.

**Right Way**

The girl is listening to the interviewer.

**Wrong Way**

The girl is not facing the interviewer and so she looks like she is not listening.

# Don't Be a Space Invader

- Keep about an arm's length away.

- Don't get too close.

# Don't be a space invader when you sit at lunch.

**Right Way**

He leaves some space between them.

**Wrong Way**

Too close. The student is being a space invader.

# Don't be a space invader when you say "Hi" in the hallway.

**Right Way**

They are at least an arm's length away.

**Wrong Way**

Too close. The boy is making the girl nervous because he is following her.

## ■ Don't be a space invader when you sit in class.

**Right Way**

The boy sits in his row, leaving space between him and the girl.

**Wrong Way**

Too close. The boy invades the girls space.

**Don't be a space invader when you use the bathroom.**

Which urinal would you use if you walked into this bathroom?

# Don't be a space invader when you use the bathroom.

**Right Way**

He uses a urinal far from the one the other person is using.

**Wrong Way**

Too close. He uses the urinal right next to another person when other urinals are available. And he seems to be looking in the direction of the other man's private parts.

# CONVERSATION RELATED SKILLS

# Greetings

- The first time during the day that you see someone you know, look at them and say "Hi, how are you?"

- When you pass someone in the hallway or see them at lunch, look at them and say "Hi."

- When someone is leaving for the day, look at them and say "Goodbye" or "See you later."

Note: with peers you can use more informal language like "What's up?" or "Later." With adults you may need to use more formal language like "Hello" and "Goodbye."

■ The first time during the day that you see someone you know, look at them and say "Hi, how are you?"

**Right Way**

The first time they see each other during the day, they say "Hi, how are you?"

**Wrong Way**

The young woman says "Hello," but the woman in the wheelchair does not look up or say anything.

24

When you pass someone in the hallway or see them at lunch, look at them and say "Hi."

**Right Way**

They all look at the girl and say "Hi."

**Wrong Way**

Nobody looks at the girl or says "Hi."

**When you pass someone in the hallway or see them at lunch, look at them and say "Hi."**

**Right Way**

They say "Hi" to each other using informal language because they are peers.

**Wrong Way**

She says "Hi" to him, but he does not look up or notice.

When someone is leaving for the day, look at them and say "Goodbye" or "See you later."

**Right Way**

The girls are leaving, so they look at the teacher and say "Goodbye."

**Wrong Way**

The girls are leaving in the middle of the teacher's conversation. They do not look at him and they use informal language, which makes them sound rude.

# Interrupting in Conversation

■ Decide if you want to interrupt because you need help or you want something.

■ Wait quietly. Try to get the other person's attention without words by gesturing with your hand, looking at them, and getting in their line of vision.

■ When there is a pause or they look at you, then say "Excuse me" and ask for what you want or need.

■ Decide if you need to interrupt because you need help or want something.

The student wants to know what he has for homework. He will need to interrupt the other two students to ask.

■ Wait quietly until they look at you. Try to get the other person's attention without words by looking at them, gesturing with your hand, and getting in their line of vision.

**Right Way**

The student does not talk. He looks at the other students and tries to get in their line of vision until they look at him.

**Wrong Way**

The student did not wait for them to finish or look at him; he just began talking.

■ When there is a pause or they look at you, then say "Excuse me" and ask for what you want or need.

**Right Way**

The student waits until they look at him, says "Excuse me" and asks about the homework.

**Wrong Way**

The student does not wait or say "Excuse me," so they are annoyed with him.

# Interrupting in Class

- Decide if you want to interrupt because you need help or you want something.

- Raise your hand and wait quietly to be called on.

- When the teacher calls on you say "Excuse me" and ask for what you want or need.

- Don't interrupt anymore if the teacher says to stop. Sometimes teachers have set times for questions and times when they do not want you to say anything.

■ Decide if you need to interrupt because you need help or want to say something.

The student is not understanding what the teacher is saying, so he will need to raise his hand to get the teacher's attention.

# Raise your hand and wait quietly to be called on.

**Right Way**

The student raises his hand and waits quietly to be called on.

**Wrong Way**

The student raised his hand but calls out and does not let the teacher finish explaining what to do.

When the teacher calls on you, say "Excuse me" and ask for what you want or need.

■ Don't interrupt anymore if the teacher says to stop. Sometimes teachers have set times for questions and times when they do not want you to say anything.

**Right Way**

The student stops asking questions until the teacher is done.

**Wrong Way**

Even though he raises his hand, the student should not keep trying to ask questions after the teacher said to stop. The teacher is getting angry.

# Interrupting at Work

■ If you need to interrupt someone who is working, quietly get their attention by knocking on the door or getting in their line of vision.

■ Wait for them to give you a signal that it is okay to interrupt (e.g., they may say "Come in").

■ Then say "Excuse me" and tell them what you need to say.

If you need to interrupt someone who is working, quietly get their attention by knocking on the door or getting in their line of vision.

The young man knocks on the door and quietly shows the woman he has a package for her.

- Wait for them to give you a signal that it is okay to interrupt (e.g., they may say "Come in").

**Right Way**

The student waits until the woman signals for him to come in.

**Wrong Way**

The student just pushes the package through the open window, interrupting the woman's phone call.

■ Wait for them to give you a signal that it is okay to interrupt (e.g., they may say "Come in").

**Right Way**

The student comes in after the woman gestures that it's okay to come in.

**Wrong Way**

He walks right into the office before she says to come in.

■ Then say "Excuse me" and tell them what you need to say.

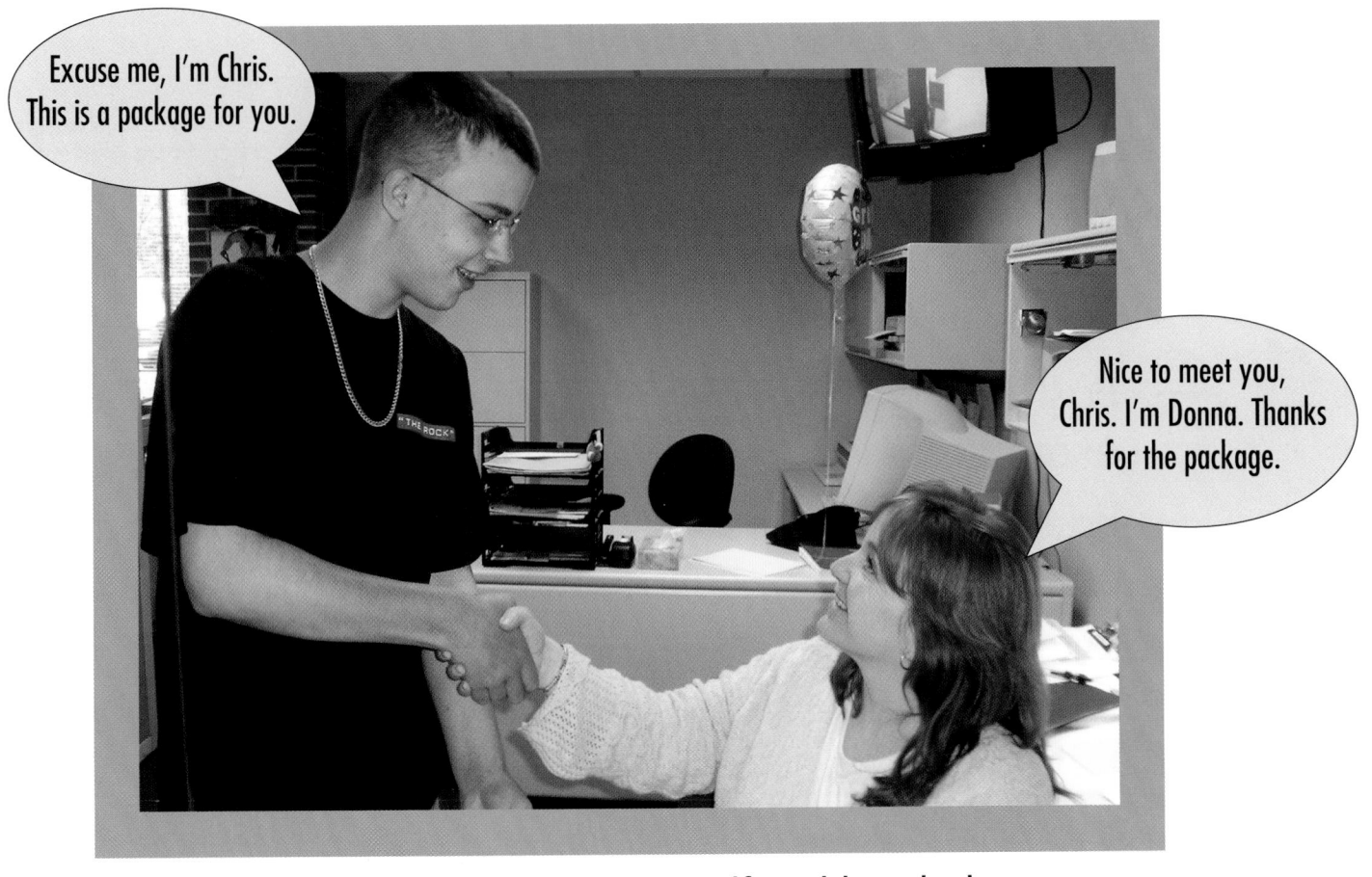

The student introduces himself and hands the
woman the package.

# Starting a Conversation with Someone You Know

■ When you see someone for the first time during the day ask, "How are you?"

■ Ask about the:

— Past: "How was _____?"
examples: class, your weekend, your vacation

— Present: "What are you _____?"
examples: doing, eating, reading, playing

— Future: "What are you going to do _____?"
examples: after school, this weekend, for vacation

— Person's interests: "How is _____?"
examples: your job, baseball practice, the play, your new video game

■ Ask (Who, What, Where, When, Why, or How) or Tell (I _____) about what they said.

When you see someone for the first time during the day ask, "How are you?"

## Ask about the past.

## Ask (Who, What, Where, When, Why, or How) or Tell (I _____) about what they said.

## Ask about the present.

## Ask (Who, What, Where, When, Why, or How) or Tell (I ____) about what they said.

When you see someone for the first time during the day ask, "How are you?"

■ Ask about the future.

■ Ask (Who, What, Where, When, Why, or How) or
Tell (I _____ ) about what they said.

When you see someone for the first time during the day ask, "How are you?"

# ■ Ask about the person's interests.

The student on the right recently got a new video game, so that's what the student on the left asks him about.

## Ask (Who, What, Where, When, Why, or How) or Tell (I ____) about what they said.

# Getting to Know Someone New

- Start the conversation:
  - Ask about something you see or might have in common (e.g. "Do you like this class?" or "That looks like a good notebook. I need one like that.")
- Introduce yourself.
- Ask and tell about these categories to get to know them and discover what you have in common:
  - SCHOOL: What classes do you take? Are they good?
  - AGE: Ask only if the person is not an adult.
  - INTERESTS: What do you do for fun? Do you like sports? Do you like music? What shows do you watch?
  - PLACE THEY LIVE: Where are you from? Is it nice there?
  - FAMILY: Do you have a big family? Any brothers, sisters, pets?
  - WORK: Are you working anywhere? What's it like?
- Avoid Sensitive Topics: Don't ask about things that might upset the other.
- End the Conversation: Explain why you need to go and say, "It was nice to meet you."

## Start the conversation about something you have in common.

The young man notices that the young woman has no food for lunch, just like him. That is something they have in common.

# Introduce yourself.

Michael introduces himself by saying, "By the way, my name is Michael. What's your name?"

# Ask and tell to get to know them. They talk about SCHOOL.

To keep the conversation going—

Ask questions:
WHO, WHAT, WHERE, WHEN, WHY, HOW,
WHAT ELSE?

Tell:
I _____
MY _____

## Ask and tell to get to know them. They talk more about SCHOOL.

To keep the conversation going—

Ask questions:
WHO, WHAT, WHERE, WHEN, WHY, HOW,
WHAT ELSE?

Tell:
I _____
MY _____

## Ask and tell to get to know them.
They find out about their GRADE and AGE.

To keep the conversation going—

Ask questions:
WHO, WHAT, WHERE, WHEN, WHY, HOW,
WHAT ELSE?

Tell:
I _____
MY _____

## Ask and tell to get to know them.
They talk about their INTERESTS.

To keep the conversation going—

Ask questions:
WHO, WHAT, WHERE, WHEN, WHY, HOW,
WHAT ELSE?

Tell:
I _____
MY _____

# Ask and tell to get to know them.
## They find out about WHERE THEY LIVE.

To keep the conversation going—

Ask questions:
WHO, WHAT, WHERE, WHEN, WHY, HOW,
WHAT ELSE?

Tell:
I _____
MY _____

61

## Ask and tell to get to know them. They find out about FAMILY.

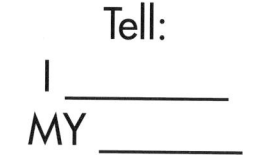

**Do you have a big family?**

**Just my parents and my brother. What about you?**

**He's 20. He's in college.**

**Just my folks. I don't have any brothers or sisters. How old is your brother?**

**Essex Community College.**

**What college?**

To keep the conversation going—

Ask questions:
WHO, WHAT, WHERE, WHEN, WHY, HOW,
WHAT ELSE?

Tell:
I _____
MY _____

## Ask and tell to get to know them. They find out about WORK.

To keep the conversation going—

Ask questions:
WHO, WHAT, WHERE, WHEN, WHY, HOW,
WHAT ELSE?

Tell:
I _____
MY _____

# Avoid sensitive topics.

**Right Way**

He compliments the young woman, saying that what she is doing is good.

**Wrong Way**

He insults the young woman, saying she is going to be poor if she does not get a job.

# ■ End the conversation.

He explains why he needs to go and says "Nice to meet you."

# Knowing When to Stop Being Funny

■ It's okay to tell jokes or try to be funny as long as all those listening like it.

■ It's important to stop trying to be funny when others ask you to stop.

■ It's not okay to keep making people laugh when it disrupts others.

■ It's okay to tell jokes or try to be funny as long as all those listening like it.

It's okay for the student to tell jokes and try to make people laugh because they all seem to be enjoying it.

■ It's important to stop trying to be funny when others
ask you to stop.

**Right Way**

The boy stops trying to tell a joke when he
finds out that the girl does not want to hear it.

**Wrong Way**

The boy continues to tell the joke after she asks
him stop. Now she is annoyed and does not
want to talk with him anymore.

## It's not okay to keep making people laugh when it disrupts others.

The boy tries to tell a joke in the middle of class. Although it may be funny to some, it is disturbing to the teacher and some of the students trying to do work.

# Ending a Conversation

■ Sometimes you may want to end a conversation because:
— You have to do something else
— You are bored.

■ Wait until you have commented or asked one question about what the other person said to show you were interested.

■ Explain why you have to go and say "Goodbye":
— If you have to do something else, say "It was nice talking to you but I have to___" (and explain what you have to do).

— If you are bored, make an excuse rather than saying you are bored, so you do not hurt their feelings. You can say you are late for class or an appointment or that you are going to get something to eat or drink.

Sometimes you may want to end a conversation because you have to do something else or you are bored.

The young man wants to end the conversation because he has to study for a test coming up.

■ Wait until you have commented or asked one question about what the other person said to show you were interested.

**Right Way**

The young man shows he is interested by asking at least one question.

**Wrong Way**

The young man just walks away while the young woman is talking to him.

# ■ Explain why you have to go, and say "Goodbye."

**Right Way**

The young man explains why he has to go.

**Right Way**

Then the young man says "Goodbye."

Sometimes you may want to end a conversation because you have to do something else or you are bored.

The teacher continues to talk to the students after the class is over, but they need to get to their next class.

■ Wait until you have commented or asked one question about what the other person said to show you were interested.

**Right Way**

The students comment on what the teacher said.

**Wrong Way**

The students tell the teacher they are bored and just walk out while he is talking.

# Explain why you have to go, and say "Goodbye."

**Right Way**

The students tell the teacher they are late for their next class so they have to go.

**Right Way**

The students say "Goodbye" to the teacher.

■ If you get angry and jealous, they may not want to be your friend anymore.

**Wrong Way**

The girl gets angry at her friend and insults her because she sat with other girls. She may lose her friend.

**Wrong Way**

Because she got angry at her friend, her friend does not want to talk with her anymore.

When you give your friends space to have other friends, they might like being with you more.

**Right Way**

The girl lets her friend be with other friends and does not intrude on them.

**Right Way**

Because she did not intrude on them, her friend realized how much she likes her and asked her to join them.

# Avoiding Sensitive Topics and Insults

■ Sensitive topics are those that may be personal or make others feel uncomfortable to talk about. Examples might be discussing a disability, someone's race, religion, or sexual preference.

— Don't bring these topics up unless the other person brings it up first.

■ Insults are remarks that hurt people's feelings. Examples might include: saying something bad about someone's looks, abilities, or family members.

— Don't ever insult others.

# Don't bring up a sensitive topic unless the other person brings it up first.

**Right Way**

Beth only speaks about Marilyn's physical condition after Marilyn brings it up first.

**Wrong Way**

Beth refers to Marilyn's physical condition without Marilyn bringing it up first.

## Don't insult others' work.

**Right Way**

Beth does not like the necklace, but she does not insult anyone. She just says it's not right for her.

**Wrong Way**

Beth does not like the necklace and insults the people who are selling it by saying bad things about the necklace.

## Don't ask about sensitive topics unless others bring them up first.

**Right Way**

The girl does not ask the boy about sensitive topics. Only when he brings up that his family is from Trinidad does she ask him about Trinidad.

**Wrong Way**

The girl asks about a sensitive topic, race and origin, which offends the boy and makes the girl sound like she might be prejudiced, assuming the boy is foreign just because he looks different from her.

# Don't insult others about their home.

**Right Way**

The boy compliments his aunt on how nice her house is.

**Wrong Way**

The boy insults his aunt about how her house looks.

# Don't insult others about the food they cook.

**Right Way**

The boy compliments his aunt on how good her food is.

**Wrong Way**

The boy insults his aunt about how her food tastes. If he did not like it, he could have just said he was not hungry.

# Showing Understanding and Empathy

■ Look for signs that others are upset, sad or angry.

■ Ask, "Are you okay? What happened?"

■ Make supportive statements:
— Tell the person you understand how they feel. Say, "It makes sense that you feel that way, given what happened."

— Share a time you had a similar experience. Say, "I know how you feel because it happened to me . . ."

— Say something positive about them or the future. "I know things will work out for you because you are so great."

— Ask if they want to do something fun to get their mind off the problem.

— Ask if there is anything you can do to help.

Look for signs that others are upset, sad or angry.

# Ask "Are you okay? What happened?"

## ◼ Make supportive statements.

He expresses his understanding of how she feels.

## Make supportive statements.

**Right Way**

He says something positive about her and the future and that makes her feel better.

**Wrong Way**

He says something negative that makes her feel worse.

93

Look for signs that others are upset, sad or angry.

# Ask "Are you okay? What happened?"

## Make supportive statements.

The young man shares a similar experience, which makes the other student feel better.

# Make supportive statements.

**Right Way**

The young man offers to help the other student, which makes him feel better.

**Wrong Way**

The young man makes fun of the other student, making him feel worse and dislike the young man.

# Don't Be the Rule Police

■ Don't tell others what to do, even if they break the rules, unless what they are doing is:

— Dangerous or

— Hurting you or others.

# Don't tell others what to do unless they are hurting you or others.

**Right Way**

The boy is wearing a hat, which is against school rules. The other students do not say anything about it because it is not hurting anyone.

**Wrong Way**

The boy does not need to tell the other boy not to wear a hat because it is not hurting anyone.

# Don't tell others what to do unless they are hurting you or others.

**Right Way**

The girl is chewing gum which is against school rules. The other students do not say anything about it because it is not hurting anyone.

**Wrong Way**

The boy does not need to tell the girl not to chew gum because it is not hurting anyone.

# Don't tell others what to do unless they are hurting you or others.

**Right Way**

The boy getting teased tells the other to stop it. You can tell people what to do if they are hurting you.

**Wrong Way**

The boy being teased does not say anything to the other boy. It's okay to ignore teasing, but sometimes it is better to tell them to stop.

# ■ Don't tell others what to do unless they are hurting you or others.

**Wrong Way**

The boy does not need to tell the other boy what work to do. He is not the teacher.

**Wrong Way**

The boy continues to be the rule police and it is making the other boy angry.

# Asserting Your Feelings

■ Wait for the right time to talk (e.g., after class).

■ Ask nicely to talk with the person.

■ Say how you feel in a calm voice: use an "I" message.
    I feel _____
    when you _____
    because _____
    I would like _____.

■ If they will not do what you want, suggest a compromise.

## The teacher says something that upsets the student.

The girl is daydreaming while the teacher is teaching.

The teacher reprimands the girl in front of the whole class.

# Step 1: Wait for the right time to talk (e.g., after class).

**Right Way**

The student waits to talk with the teacher privately, after class.

**Wrong Way**

The student insults the teacher. She will get in more trouble and the teacher will be less likely to do what she wants.

# Step 2: Ask nicely if you can talk to the person.

**Right Way**

The student asks in a calm way to talk with the teacher.

**Wrong Way**

The student clenches her fist while she uses angry words to talk with him. She will get in more trouble and the teacher may be more likely to embarrass her again.

# Step 3: Say how you feel in a calm voice. Use an "I" message.

**Right Way**

The student tells how she feels and what she wants in a calm way.

**Wrong Way**

The student threatens to scream at the teacher. She will get in more trouble and the teacher will be less likely to do what she wants.

## Step 4: If they will not do what you want, suggest a compromise.

**Right Way**

The student accepts she can't have everything she wants, so she suggests a compromise.

**Wrong Way**

The student does not accept that it is the teacher's job to keep her attention. Her angry actions may get her in trouble with the principal.

108

# Giving Criticism

■ Only criticize or complain to someone if they are doing something that directly bothers you or is dangerous to others. Otherwise, don't say anything.

■ If you have to complain about what someone is doing, use a calm voice and explain what you want them to do. You might use an "I" message.

I feel _____

when you _____

because _____.

I want _____.

Only criticize or complain to someone if they are doing something that directly bothers you or is dangerous to others. Otherwise don't say anything.

**Right Way**

The boy on the left is biting his nails. Even though the boy on the right thinks it is disgusting, he does not complain because it is not directly bothering him.

**Wrong Way**

The boy on the left is biting his nails. Even though it is not directly bothering him, the boy on the right shouts insults.

If you have to complain about what someone is doing, use a calm voice and explain what you want them to do. You might use an "I" message.

**Right Way**

In a nice tone of voice, the boy uses an "I" message to tell the other boy to stop whispering.

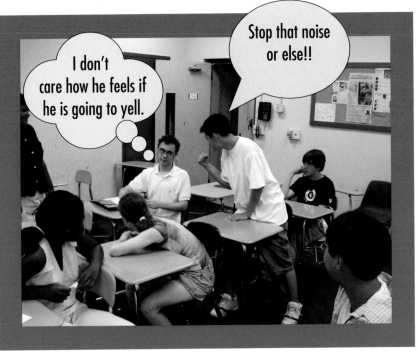

**Wrong Way**

Instead of talking in a nice tone, the boy screams for the other boy to stop and threatens him. He may get in trouble with the teacher or others.

# Conflict Resolution

■ When you are upset with others, try to schedule a time to talk with them rather than confronting them without warning.

■ When they are ready to talk, tell them in a calm voice what upset you. You can use an "I" message as a positive way to tell them your concern:
  I felt _____ when _____.
  I want _____.

■ Then listen to their side without interrupting. Check to see if you understood what they said.

■ While taking turns talking, offer solutions that might work for both of you until you can come to some agreement.

When you are upset with others, try to schedule a time to talk with them rather than confronting them without warning.

**Right Way**

One girl asks the other girl if they can schedule a time to talk. Because she was calm, she succeeded in finding a time to talk.

**Wrong Way**

The first girl starts yelling at the other girl about what upset her. This makes the other girl run away.

■ When they are ready to talk, tell them in a calm voice what upset you. You can use an "I" message as a positive way to tell them your concern.

Thanks for talking with me. I felt upset when I heard that you told people I was a bully. I want to know if you really said that or think that.

**Right Way**

The girl calmly tells the other girls what upset her using an "I" message: I felt _____, when __ _____. I want _____. By being calm, the other girl was able to listen.

You told everyone that I am bully. That makes you a bully!

I didn't even say that! Now you <u>are</u> a bully! Get away from me!

**Wrong Way**

The girl starts yelling at the other girl about what upset her. She also insults her. When you yell and insult others, they won't listen.

# Then listen to their side without interrupting. Check to see if you understood what they said.

**Right Way**

The girl listens to the response of the other girl without interrupting. When they listen to each other, they may clear up misunderstandings and solve the problem.

**Wrong Way**

The girls interrupt and insult each other without listening to each other. This will not solve anything.

While taking turns talking, offer solutions that might work for both of you until you can come to some agreement.

## Right Way

The girls understand each other because they listened to each other.
So they begin to offer solutions to the problem.

# The girls solved the problem.

# Dealing with Teasing

- Ask if the person was kidding.

- Tell them calmly, but firmly, to stop.

- If they do not stop, say you do not care what they say and walk away.

- If they continue to tease or follow you, go tell an adult, teacher, parent, or supervisor.

## ■ Ask if the person was kidding.

Sometimes people are just kidding and do not mean to hurt your feelings. If you tell them to stop they may even say they are sorry.

# Tell them calmly, but firmly, to stop.

**Right Way**

The student tells the teaser to stop in a calm firm voice. His calmness suggests that the teasing is not really getting to him, so the teaser may stop.

**Wrong Way**

The teaser sees that the student is getting angry so he may tease him more now.

120

■ If they do not stop, say you do not care what they say, and walk away.

By ignoring him and walking away, the student makes the teaser think he does not care, and the teaser may stop trying to make him angry.

If they continue to tease or follow you, go tell an adult, teacher, parent, or supervisor.

He continues to get teased.

So he tells a teacher.

# The teaser gets in trouble.

The teaser gets in trouble because he did not stop teasing despite being asked to stop and being warned by a teacher.

# Asking Someone Out on a Date

■ Start a conversation, introduce yourself and get to know them first by asking about things you might have in common.
(See "Getting to Know Someone New," pp. 54-65.)

■ If they seem welcoming, talk to them again to find out more about them.

■ Compliment them and do something nice for them.

■ If they continue to seem welcoming, then suggest getting together with them based on a common interest.

Start a conversation, introduce yourself and get to know them first by asking about things you might have in common.

The young man recognizes the young woman from his math class. That is something they have in common.

**Start a conversation, introduce yourself and get to know them first by asking about things you might have in common.**

Michael introduces himself by saying, "My name is Michael. What's your name?"

Start a conversation, introduce yourself and get to know them first by asking about things you might have in common.

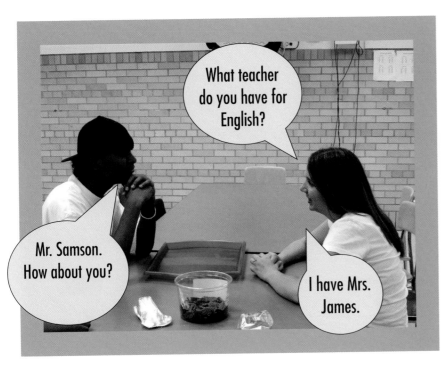

To keep the conversation going—

Ask questions:
WHO, WHAT, WHERE, WHEN, WHY, HOW,
WHAT ELSE?

Tell:
I _____
MY _____

**Start a conversation, introduce yourself and get to know them first by asking about things you might have in common.**

To keep the conversation going—

Ask questions:

WHO, WHAT, WHERE, WHEN, WHY, HOW,
WHAT ELSE?

Tell:

I _____

MY _____

■ If they seem welcoming, talk to them again to find out more about them.

**Right Way**

He says hello from a distance to see if she is interested. She seems welcoming because she looks at him, smiles and says hello back.

**Wrong Way**

As Michael follows Sheila, she turns away from him and looks upset, indicating she does not want to talk with him. He should stop following her.

# If they seem welcoming, talk to them again to find out more about them.

**Welcoming**

She is facing him and smiling suggesting she enjoys talking with him, so he continues to talk with her.

**Welcoming**

She leans back on her locker rather than going to her next class. This seems to indicate that she wants to stay and talk with him.

# Compliment them and do something nice for them.

He compliments her.

He offers to do something nice for her.

■ If they continue to seem welcoming, then suggest getting together with them based on a common interest.

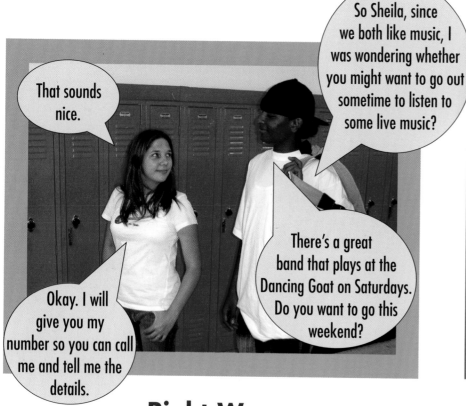

**Right Way**

Sheila seems welcoming because she turns to him and smiles. So he suggests getting together.

**Wrong Way**

Sheila does not look welcoming, she turns away and looks upset. Michael should stop following her and asking her out, before he gets in trouble.

# DEALING WITH SCHOOL AND WORK RELATED SKILLS

# Dealing with the Fear of Trying Something New

- Tell someone you are feeling fearful, rather than acting angry and refusing to do the work.

- Ask if you can watch others first, until you feel more confident.

- Remember, it's normal to be fearful the first time you do something, but the more you try it, the easier it will get.

- Try to do some of it.

- Think about what you learned. Maybe it was not as bad as you thought.

The teacher tells him it is his turn to present in front of the class.

# Tell someone you are feeling fearful, rather than acting angry and refusing to do the work.

**Right Way**

When he tells the teacher that he is nervous, the teacher wants to help him.

**Wrong Way**

When he refuses to do the work, the teacher just thinks he is trying to be defiant to get out of the work.

## Ask if you can watch others first, until you feel more confident.

**Right Way**

When he asks to watch others first, the teacher allows it, understanding that this might help the student.

**Wrong Way**

When he walks out, he is going to get in trouble.

Remember, it's normal to be fearful the first time you do something, but the more you try it, the easier it will get.

While he watches the other student go first, he remembers that he usually feels better after he tries something, even if he is nervous at first.

# Try to do some of it.

The teacher tells him to try it now.

He tries it. He presents in front of others.

He realizes that he really had no reason to be afraid.

# Trying When It's Hard

■ Try to do the work.

■ Ask for help if you need it.

■ Negotiate or compromise rather than refusing to do the work.

■ Ask for a short break if you get upset.

■ Go back to doing your work.

# The instructor gives the student work to do.

# Try to do the work.

**Right Way**

He tries it.

**Wrong Way**

He crumples the paper in anger.

# ■ Ask for help if you need it.

**Right Way**

He asks for help when he has trouble.

**Wrong Way**

He gets angry when he has trouble.

# Negotiate or compromise rather than refusing to do the work.

**Right Way**

The young man negotiates to do some of the work.

**Wrong Way**

The young man gets angry when he has trouble.

# Ask for a break if you need one.

He asks for a short break.

He takes a five-minute break.

# Come back and try again.

He comes back to do his work after
the break is over.

The instructor is impressed with his efforts.

# Accepting No or Waiting For What You Want

- Sometimes parents and people say "No" when you ask them for something.

- Say "Okay" and do not get angry.

- If you accept "No" then the other person will be happy and may let you do something you want to do later.

- If you get angry and refuse to wait, you probably will not get what you want.

Sometimes people say "No" when you ask them for something.

When the boy asks to watch TV, his mother says "No" and tells him to do his work first.

# Say "Okay" and do not get angry.

**Right Way**

He says "Okay" and does not get angry.
He knows he will get to watch TV later.

**Right Way**

He gets his work done so he can have time to
watch TV.

If you accept "No" then the other person will be happy and may let you do something you want to do later.

**Right Way**

He now gets to watch TV because he finished his work.

■ **If you get angry and refuse to wait, you probably will not get what you want.**

**Wrong Way**

He argues with his mother. This will not get him what he wants.

**Wrong Way**

He threatens his mother. This will not get him what he wants and may cause him to lose TV privileges for a longer period of time.

# If you get angry and refuse to wait, you probably will not get what you want.

## Consequences of the Wrong Way

His mother unplugs the TV and takes it away because of the angry way her son spoke to her.

He lost his TV privileges for the whole evening because he refused to wait until he was done with his work to watch TV and he argued with his mother.

# Dealing with Mistakes

- Tell yourself, "It's okay to make mistakes, that's how we learn. The sooner I correct them, the sooner I will be done."

- Ask for help if you need it.

- Try it again.

- Be proud of yourself for fixing your mistake.

■ Tell yourself, "It's okay to make mistakes, that's how we learn. The sooner I correct them, the sooner I will be done."

**Right Way**

The young woman knows it's okay to make mistakes, and she wants to correct them now so she can go to lunch sooner.

**Wrong Way**

The girl cannot accept that she made a mistake. Being upset will cause her to take longer to fix the mistake and get to lunch.

# Ask for help if you need it.

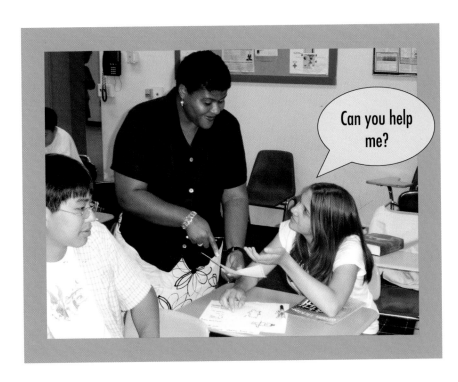

**Right Way**

The young woman asks for help instead of getting angry.

**Wrong Way**

The young woman gets angry instead of asking for help.

## ■ Try it again.

### Right Way
The young woman tries to do the work again.

### Wrong Way
The young woman gets so angry she wants to quit.

# Be proud of yourself for fixing your mistake.

# Working with Others—Compromising

- When you have to work with others, it is more important to get along than to have it all your way. First, find out what the other people want to do.

- Tell them what you want to do.

- Be respectful of others' opinions as you decide what you will do.

  — Speak positively when you try to convince others of your idea: "I like your idea but I think this would be even better because…"

  — Try to compromise: do a little of what both of you want to do.

# The teacher tells the class they have small group projects to complete.

The teacher tells the class about the project.

The teacher tells the two students they need to work together.

When you have to work with others, it is more important to get along than to have it all your way. First, find out what the other person wants to do.

**Right Way**

She asks him what he wants to do.

**Wrong Way**

She tells him what to do. He will not want to work with her if she is demanding.

# ■ Tell them what you want to do.

**Right Way**

Now she says what she wants to do.

**Wrong Way**

She won't say what she wants to do. The project cannot continue without her ideas.

■ Be respectful of others' opinions as you decide what you will do. Speak positively when you try to convince others of your idea.

**Right Way**

He shows respect for her opinion as he tries to convince her to do it a different way.

**Wrong Way**

She insults him and insists on her way. Now the project might not get done because they cannot get along.

■ Be respectful of others' opinions as you decide what you will do. Try to compromise: do a little of what both of you want to do.

**Right Way**

She suggests a compromise to use both their ideas. Now both are happy.

**Wrong Way**

She refuses to compromise, so now the project cannot get done. Both have to be willing to compromise to get things done.

# When they compromise, they get their work done.

# Job Interviewing

- Dress neatly for the interview, wearing suitable clothing such as buttoned shirts, nice shoes, dress-pants (or dresses for women); no jeans or sneakers.

- Introduce yourself to the interviewer with eye contact and a firm handshake.

- Wait for the interviewer to tell you where to sit.

- Present a good listening position (eye contact, good posture, facing the speaker).

- Answer questions, pointing out positive traits about yourself, and make complimentary statements about the employer. Avoid saying negative things about yourself or them.

- Wait for the interviewer to indicate that the interview is over, then thank them for meeting with you and shake their hand.

- Later, send them a letter thanking them again for the interview, and mention your desire to work for them.

■ Dress neatly for the interview, wearing suitable clothing such as buttoned shirts, nice shoes, dress-pants (or dresses for women); no jeans or sneakers.

**Right Way**

The student is wearing a buttoned shirt, tie, and dress-pants. The interviewer will think he cares about the job.

**Wrong Way**

The student is wearing pants rolled up with an untucked shirt. The interviewer will think he does not care about the job.

# Introduce yourself to the interviewer with eye contact and a firm handshake.

### Right Way

The student introduces himself, looks the interviewer in the eyes, smiles and shakes her hand.

### Wrong Way

The student does not look at, shake hands with, or introduce himself to the interviewer. The interviewer may think he does not care about the job.

# Wait for the interviewer to tell you where to sit.

**Right Way**

The student waits for the interviewer to tell him where to sit.

**Wrong Way**

The student sits in the interviewer's chair without waiting to be told where to sit.

- Present a good listening position (eye contact, good posture, facing the speaker).

**Right Way**

The student faces the interviewer and his posture (leaning forward slightly) makes him seem interested.

**Wrong Way**

The student does not face the speaker. He seems to be looking down and uninterested in the interview.

■ Answer questions, pointing out positive traits about yourself, and make complimentary statements about the employer. Avoid saying negative things about yourself or them.

**Right Way**

The student says positive things about himself and compliments the interviewer's store.

**Wrong Way**

The student says negative things about himself and the interviewer's store.

■ Answer questions, pointing out positive traits about yourself, and make complimentary statements about the employer. Avoid saying negative things about yourself or them.

### Right Way

The student has not had a paying job so he tells about his positive volunteer work experience, which is very relevant to the job.

### Wrong Way

The student says in a sad voice that he has never worked. He leaves out the positive information about his volunteer experience.

■ Answer questions, pointing out positive traits about yourself, and make complimentary statements about the employer. Avoid saying negative things about yourself or them.

**Right Way**

The student takes this opportunity to enthusiastically say many positive things about himself and again compliment the interviewer's store.

**Wrong Way**

The student says nothing positive and looks away. He leaves the interviewer wondering why she should hire this student who does not seem interested.

■ Answer questions, pointing out positive traits about yourself, and make complimentary statements about the employer. Avoid saying negative things about yourself or them.

**Right Way**

The student does not reveal real weaknesses. Being a perfectionist is really a strength. And saying he wants to continue to improve serving customers means that he is already good at it.

**Wrong Way**

The student reveals negative things about himself that may make the interviewer not want to hire him.

■ Wait for the interviewer to indicate that the interview is over, then thank them for meeting with you and shake their hand.

**Right Way**

The student waits for the interviewer to rise and extend her hand, then the student shakes her hand and thanks her for the interview.

**Wrong Way**

He gets up before the interviewer and starts to walk out without saying "Thank you."

■ Later, send them a letter thanking them again for the interview and mention your desire to work for them.

Dear Mrs. Johnson,

Thank you very much for meeting with me to discuss the job at your wonderful bookstore. I continue to be very interested in the position and look forward to hearing from you. I can be reached at (973) 555-1212.

Sincerely,
Paul Miller

# Extend teaching and learning with these other great resources by Dr. Jed Baker!

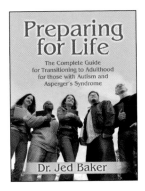

This resource offers 73 skill lessons for older kids, targeting communication, anger/anxiety management, social skills, and employment-related skills. The lessons and activities sync up perfectly with the topics and photos in *The Social Skills Picture Book for High School and Beyond*.

ISBN 9781932565331    $34.95

Dr. Baker brings his strategies to life, with more than four hours of valuable information! Learn how to: build an individual's social skills in crucial areas, develop an effective behavior plan, manage and prevent meltdowns, help create peer acceptance, and assess social skills of individuals or groups.

ISBN 9781932565539    $99.95

Jed provides 70 skill lessons that focus on social-communication issues in school-age children. Each lesson includes activities to help students practice the skill at home or at school.

ISBN 9781931282208    $34.95

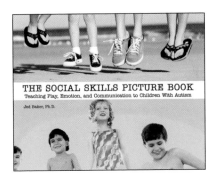

Winner of an iParenting Media Award, this book shows photos of younger students in real-life social situations, along with guidance on the right and wrong ways to react.

ISBN 9781885477910    $39.95

Dr. Baker teamed up with musician and certified music therapist Jeffrey Friedberg to create 16 original songs that teach invaluable social skills such as sharing, taking turns, making friends, and more!

$14.95

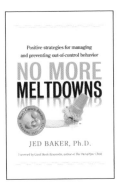

Award-winning author Dr. Jed Baker offers an easy-to-follow, four-step model that will improve your everyday relationships with the children in your life.

ISBN 9781932565621    $14.95

Available at fine retailers everywhere, or at www.FHautism.com.